Disability and Inclusive Communities

CALVIN SHORTS

A series published by the Calvin College Press
Titles in the Calvin Shorts Series:

Emerging Adulthood and Faith

The Church and Religious Persecution

Christians and Cultural Difference

American Roots

Does the Reformation Still Matter?

When Helping Heals

Congregations, Neighborhoods, Places

Sport. Faith. Life.

Disability and Inclusive Communities

Disability and Inclusive Communities

Kevin Timpe

Calvin PRESS
COLLEGE
Grand Rapids, MI • calvin.edu/press

Published 2018 by the Calvin College Press
3201 Burton St. SE
Grand Rapids, MI 49546

Scripture quotations are from the Holy Bible, New International Version®. NIV®. Copyright © 1973, 1978, 1984, 2011 by Biblica, Inc.™ Used by permission of Zondervan. All rights reserved worldwide. www.zondervan.com. The "NIV" and "New International Version" are trademarks registered in the United States Patent and Trademark Office by Biblica, Inc.™

Publisher's Cataloging-in-Publication Data

Names: Timpe, Kevin, author.
Title: Disability and inclusive communities / Kevin Timpe.
Series: Calvin Shorts
Description: Includes bibliographical references. | Grand Rapids, MI: Calvin College Press, 2018.
Identifier: LCCN 2018960029 | ISBN 978-1-937555-32-0 (pbk.) | 978-1-937555-33-7 (ebook)
Subjects: LCSH Disability awareness. | Disability—Social aspects. | People with disabilities. | Inclusive education. | Social integration. | Christian life. | BISAC FAMILY & RELATIONSHIPS / Children with Special Needs | SOCIAL SCIENCE / People with Disabilities | RELIGION / Christian Life / Relationships
Classification: LCC HV1568.T56 2018 | DDC 305.9/08—dc23

Cover design: Robert Alderink
Interior design and typeset: Katherine Lloyd, The DESK

The Calvin College Press has no responsibility for the persistence or accuracy of URLs for external or third-party internet websites referred to in this publication and does not guarantee that any content on such websites is, or will remain, accurate or appropriate.

Dedicated to Jameson,
Samuel,
Asher,
Jack,
Mathilda,
Benjamin,
Carlyle,
Antonio,
Elizabeth,
Joe,
Cassaundra,
Isaac,
Ezra,
Christian,
Madison,
Jordan,
Vaiya,
Lainey,
Raelin,
Eivind,
Braxton,
Rae,
Greyson,
Isabella,
Ava,

Michele,
Owen,
Heidi,
Laura,
Patrice,
Joshua,
Tara,
Christopher,
Aidan,
Heather,
Luke,
David,
Edmund,
Vicente,
Matthias,
Peter,
Nathanial,
Annie,
Miles,
Sebastian,
Alana,
David,
Freddie,
Philip,

and all those who love them.

Contents

Series Editor's Foreword 9

Additional Resources 11

Acknowledgments 13

1 Learning to Care, Learning to Notice 15

2 The History of Exclusion 31

3 Structural Exclusion 47

4 Interpersonal Exclusion 61

5 Social Challenges 77

6 Moving Forward 95

Notes 109

For Further Reading 115

Series Editor's Foreword

> *Midway along the journey of our life*
> . *I woke to find myself in some dark woods,*
> *For I had wandered off from the straight path.*

So begins *The Divine Comedy*, a classic meditation on the Christian life, written by Dante Alighieri in the fourteenth century.

Dante's three images—a journey, a dark forest, and a perplexed pilgrim—still feel familiar today, don't they?

We can readily imagine our own lives as a series of journeys: not just the big journey from birth to death, but also all the little trips from home to school, from school to job, from place to place, from old friends to new. In fact, we often feel we are simultaneously on multiple journeys that tug us in diverse and sometimes opposing directions. We recognize those dark woods from fairy tales and nightmares and the all-too-real conundrums that crowd our everyday lives. No wonder we frequently feel perplexed. We wake up shaking our heads, unsure if we know how to live wisely today or tomorrow or next week.

This series has in mind just such perplexed pilgrims. Each book invites you, the reader, to walk alongside experienced guides who will help you understand the contours of the road as well as the surrounding landscape. They will cut back the underbrush, untangle myths and misconceptions, and suggest ways to move forward.

And they will do it in books intended to be read in an evening or during a flight. Calvin Shorts are designed not just for perplexed pilgrims but also for busy ones. We live in a complex and changing world. We need nimble ways to acquire knowledge, skills, and wisdom. These books are one way to meet those needs.

John Calvin, after whom this series is named, recognized our pilgrim condition. "We are always on the road," he said, and although this road, this life, is full of perplexities, it is also "a gift of divine kindness which is not to be refused." Calvin Shorts takes as its starting point this claim that we are called to live well in a world that is both gift and challenge.

In *The Divine Comedy*, Dante's guide is Virgil, a wise but not omniscient mentor. So, too, the authors in the Calvin Shorts series don't pretend to know it all. They, like you and me, are pilgrims. And they invite us to walk with them as together we seek to live more faithfully in this world that belongs to God.

Susan M. Felch
Executive Editor
The Calvin College Press

Additional Resources

Additional online resources for *Disability and Inclusive Communities* may be available at www.calvin.edu/press.

Additional information, references, and citations are included in the notes at the end of this book. Rather than using footnote numbers, the comments are keyed to phrases and page numbers.

Acknowledgments

Publishing a book, like living, is much more communal than we often realize. The folks at the Calvin College Press have been wonderful to work with. Susan Felch not only encouraged me to take on this project but also has been a helpful, light-handed, and trusting editor throughout. Dale Williams, too, was spectacular to work with. Thanks to him especially for helping make the cover happen. Melinda Timmer was a meticulous copy editor who smoothed over and improved many parts of my text. Michaela Osborne oversaw the publication process with efficiency and grace. Barb Newman is an incarnation of the kind of community I long for, and her vision has shaped me and many others. In the midst of her many travels, she provided comments on the penultimate draft for the press, comments that helped me avoid a number of errors.

Much of the material in this book was given a trial run in a spring 2018 course on disability that I taught for the Calvin Academy for Lifelong Learning. Thanks to all my colleagues in the philosophy department who trust me with my research and encouraged me to write for the Church and not just the guild.

I am grateful for Debra Buursma, Nate Clark, Tom Hoeksema, Andrew Low, Sam Read, Cassaundra Wolf, and Audrey Yap, all of whom graciously gave me helpful comments and suggestions on earlier drafts of the manuscript. The book is better for their input. Carlyle King not only gave me comments but also has greatly influenced how I think about inclusive communities through countless conversations. My dear friend, I wish this book wasn't needed.

Allison, my wife, has lived the journey described in this book with me, and her influence and patience are interwoven throughout these pages. We all know that I have no natural patience of my own. Our daughters, Emmaline and Maggie, are paragons of how to love people with disabilities, and I have learned from their gentleness and openness. And none of this book could be what it is without Jameson. He inspires me, motivates me, and rewards me with snuggles daily.

Disability and Inclusive Communities is underwritten by the Calvin Institute of Christian Worship and the Teacher Education and Graduate Studies in Education programs at Calvin College.

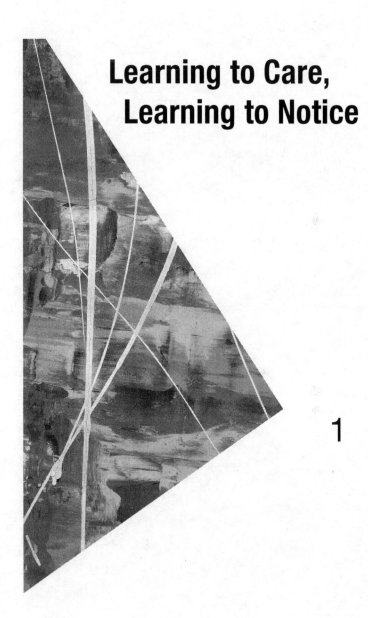

Learning to Care,
Learning to Notice

1

I didn't set out to be a disability advocate. I just wanted to be a good father to our son. But I have come to learn that being a good father to him means that I need to be an advocate. And I have also learned that being an advocate isn't just something I need to do as an expression and form of love for our son. It is something I need to do as an act of love for our whole family—for our son, our two daughters, and my wife. And as my advocacy has spread, I have realized that it is also something I need to do for other individuals with disabilities and for their families.

We sometimes think that when we have helped another person, we have helped only *that person*. But I have learned that the whole community is better off when we welcome individuals with disabilities into our lives. If you are a reader who has a disability, I hope you know you make the lives of those around you better. We all live better lives when we structure our communities in ways that include rather than exclude. When we help individuals in our communities, we improve our communities.

In a nutshell, that is the central theme of this book. We are all better off when we include rather than exclude individuals with disabilities.

But before I elaborate on that theme, let me first tell you some of our story.

MEETING JAMESON

As those of you who are parents know, parenting is hard. First-time parenting is, in at least a number of ways, harder. For with the first child, everything is new.

Our first child was a son. Unlike many parents these days, we didn't find out the sex of our child until he—*he*, a boy!—was born. His birth was wonderful. And exciting. And scary. Allison, my wife, had gone a week past her due date with still no indications of labor. So she was admitted into the hospital for a scheduled induction. We went in with the kind of reckless confidence that characterizes people who don't know exactly what they are getting into.

As we had been instructed in our birthing class, we went in with a plan. Unfortunately, what we had planned for didn't happen. In the middle of the night, Allison had to go on oxygen, as our child's heart rate kept dropping. After approximately sixteen hours of labor, the doctor came in and said that he was going to do a C-section. Given that it was 6 a.m. and the family who had come to town to help us was still asleep at our house about ten miles away, I asked the doctor if it could wait a half hour or so for our family to arrive. He said, "No. This needs to happen. Immediately!"

Thirteen minutes later, I was holding our son. The next day we named him Jameson. Jameson Lloyd Cooper Timpe—a name fit for a lawyer or an accountant like his mother and grandfather. He was glorious. He was ours.

But in those first few days, we noticed he had a few physical "quirks." None of these were themselves major or indicative of problems. But a few weeks later we would learn that a number of them often correlate with genetic abnormalities. We talked his doctors into doing a genetic screening. They found that he has a translocation on chromosomes 5 and 6—basically, parts of those chromosomes played Red Rover and switched locations. Part of one copy of chromosome 5 is on chromosome 6; part of what is supposed to be on that copy of chromosome 6 is instead on chromosome 5. We were referred to a geneticist to have a more fine-grained test. Through it we found that in addition to the translocation, our son has a deletion on one copy of chromosome 2; that is, he is missing a bit of material, and so that copy of chromosome 2 is incomplete.

Supposedly, these two genetic abnormalities are unrelated. We were told by the geneticist, "It's like your son was struck by lightning twice." When we received this diagnosis, the geneticist told us that there were no previously diagnosed cases of this particular deletion in the medical literature. We had a diagnosis, but we didn't have a prognosis. Not until about seven years later would we discover that in the intervening years a number of other individuals with the same deletion had also been diagnosed. As of this writing, there are at least fifty-three cases in the medical literature. We have even talked with other parents of individuals with the same condition. And we now know that it is possible for someone with our son's condition to live into their thirties, perhaps even longer. We finally have at least a partial prognosis.

When we received Jameson's official diagnosis—he has 2p15-16.1 Microdeletion syndrome—he had already been receiving physical therapy for wry neck, a tilt of the head that in his case was congenital. It was likely caused, at least in part, by his genetic condition. He has been in therapy—physical, occupational, speech, social—for all but the first six weeks of his life. He is now ten. There is no part of his life that Jameson remembers that doesn't involve therapy.

DAY-TO-DAY IMPACT

When Jameson was five years old, I was interviewed for a wonderful blog, *This Little Miss Miggy Stayed Home*. Miggy (not her real name) and her husband have three children, the second of whom was born with limb differences. Miggy runs a series of "Special Needs Spotlights" on her blog where she interviews parents of children with disabilities. A few of her interviews are with individuals with disabilities themselves rather than with parents. Miggy's interviews follow a fairly consistent pattern. She has the parent introduce the entire family and talk a bit about what the disability in question is. She asks about the personality of the child and if there are any funny conversations or moments the family has had because of the disability. One of the questions she regularly asks is "How does your child's disability affect your day-to-day life?" Here is part of what I answered:

> This is hard to answer—it's a question we've been asked quite a few times in meetings with therapists—because Jameson is our oldest and there's not really any aspect of life that it doesn't impact. . . . We can do most things in life, but it takes more time, more energy, and more patience—the latter, I'm sad to say, doesn't come naturally to me. Even tonight, going trick-or-treating with our friends, we had to go much slower than the rest because of how hard it is for him to walk. I know it's a small thing, and I certainly understand that the others don't need to walk slowly with us, but it's hard for me to see him miss out on even some of these details of life.

(I tell more of this story of trick-or-treating in chapter 4.) The question of how Jameson's disability affects our lives is still hard to answer all these years later. There is no part of his life—of our lives—that is free from its effects. The exact nature of the impact, however, has changed over the years. His speech delay has improved, and he is now able to communicate in ways that used to be a serious struggle. We celebrate this development, given that approximately 60% of individuals with his underlying genetic condition never develop significant speech.

Jameson received an Autism Spectrum Disorder (ASD) diagnosis a few years later. Approximately 30% of individuals with his deletion syndrome also have an ASD diagnosis. The exact correlation may be higher, as the impact of the deletion—particularly for those who are more impaired by the condition than Jameson is—may mask some of the symptoms of ASD. Jameson has many of the social impairments that others who have autism often have. He struggles with eye contact and reciprocal speech, particularly with people he doesn't know. He would rather play by himself than with most people, even though he is extremely social with his sisters and parents. He can be hyperfocused on certain tasks and stims, which are self-stimulatory repetitive behaviors.

SCHOOL: THE FIRST SYSTEMIC FAILURE

One of the biggest struggles we have faced so far came when he started school. We were nervous, but trusting, when he started kindergarten. Because of his disability, the district did not want him to go to the elementary school we could see from our back porch. They wanted him to go to a different school a few miles away where he could be in a classroom with other children with disabilities. Not knowing any better—as I said, we were trusting—we agreed. While technically in kindergarten, he spent most of his school day not in the kindergarten class but in the Extended Resource Room—the "Special Ed" room. But we really liked his teacher, and he made academic and social progress that year.

About a month into first grade, Allison and Tammy—a family friend who has a son with Down syndrome who was good friends with Jameson at this time—went to a local Down syndrome society meeting. This meeting was focused on education. The two of them learned that the school and district weren't following best practices for how to educate students with disabilities. Beyond that, they were also violating state and federal law, particularly the Individuals with Disabilities Education Act. (I talk more about the Individuals with Disabilities Education Act, also referred to as IDEA, in chapter 3.) Allison and Tammy came back from that meeting heartbroken. Neither the school nor the district that we had trusted to do what was best for our children was doing what they were supposed to be doing. We realized that we had to do something. So we found the state special education manual. We read it. We learned how to make the law work for us. And then we pressured the school to follow that law.

It wasn't a fun experience. But in the course of about a year and a half, we got the district to change its policy from busing students with disabilities to a few schools to letting them attend their neighborhood schools. We got our sons to be included in a classroom with students without disabilities for most of their time at school. We got aides hired to help them as needed. In short, we advocated for our children.

And word began spreading. I was asked by other parents to help advocate for their children in their schools. For me, doing this work, even for families I didn't know, was an issue of justice. It is something that I care very much about. As the work began growing, we decided to start an advocacy nonprofit: 22 Advocacy. The logo reflects the missing bit on one copy of Jameson's second chromosome.

In the years since then, I have advocated for dozens of students and helped train parents across the country, from Maine to California.

BECOMING ADVOCATES

We didn't set out to be parents of a child with disabilities. We didn't set out to be disability advocates. But because we became the former, we realized we needed to become the latter. Over the years, as we have watched our son grow and encounter repeated difficulties, we have seen how many of his struggles aren't caused just by his disabilities. Some of the struggles he faces are caused by ways that our communities exclude rather than include individuals with disabilities. In the pages to come, I will show how we can—and should—make our communities more inclusive. And I will show how when our communities are inclusive, we *all* benefit, not just those, like our son, with disabilities.

The history of how we have mistreated members of our communities who have disabilities shows that despite our best intentions, we often get things very wrong. In the past, we routinely institutionalized individuals with disabilities. They were sent away to residential facilities, where they often had little to no engagement with the general population. This practice shows that we can harm the very people we intend to help if we don't do it right. If you have a disability, or have a family member who does, you have probably seen firsthand how good intentions can go wrong like this.

One of the primary reasons we have failed to treat individuals with disabilities well is that those of us who do not have disabilities think we know what is best for those of us who do. The disability rights movement, which began in the late 1960s, adopted this rallying cry: "nothing about us without us." Those in the movement wanted the people making decisions about people with disabilities to consult those who have them. Racial minorities often better understand racism than those who are in the racial majority. Women often better understand sexism and misogyny than men because they have firsthand knowledge of such mistreatment. Similarly, those with disabilities often better understand their struggles and exclusion than the nondisabled. But having a disability doesn't mean you can't exclude others. People with a visible disability can, for instance, forget that some disabilities are invisible and leave out those who have them. If you are reading this and have a disability yourself, I hope you will still be able to learn some ways to make your community more inclusive, both for yourself and for those around you.

I want to be clear here at the beginning. I am a non-disabled person. Other than a very minor version of dyslexia—one so minor it didn't affect me educationally—I don't have a disability. I am well aware that I am in an awkward, perhaps even dangerous, position to write a book on disability. I have the best of intentions. But as I said a few paragraphs back, history is full of harm done to individuals with disabilities by well-meaning individuals who claimed to speak for them. I have taken steps to guard against speaking for others without their consent. I had numerous friends with different kinds of disabilities read the manuscript for this book. I drew on previous writing and thinking of individuals with disabilities throughout the project. But there are also places where I am silent. There are parts of our family story that I don't tell here, because those parts aren't mine to tell. They are our son's. And if those parts are ever told, that should be his decision.

So even in telling our story, I have had to make judgments about what to include.

There is an additional danger that I am also concerned about. Not only do I not have a disability myself, but I am also the parent of a young child with disabilities. Lamar Hardwick refers to himself as "the autistic pastor." In the foreword to his book *I Am Strong*, award-winning speaker, author, and advocate Kerry Magro wrote the following:

> The popular image of autism is with children. With that we must understand that children with autism become adults with autism and we must be ready for them. Autism and other disabilities don't just stop in childhood. . . . We live in a community where the emphasis is on early intervention and children with autism, so many times adults don't get the acknowledgement they deserve.

Much of our culture's interest in disability focuses on children with disabilities, despite the fact that over 90% of Americans with disabilities are adults. There is a danger of infantilizing, or treating as children, adults with disabilities. And so in addition to the danger of my speaking for individuals with disabilities, there is another danger: because much of my own experience and advocacy have been with children, I may misunderstand some of the particular struggles and issues that adults with disabilities face.

WHY THIS BOOK?

In light of these dangers, why have I taken on this project?

First, because it is important. Disability is one of those topics that much of our culture would prefer to ignore rather than confront head on. This approach is one that harms both individuals and our communities as a whole, or so I will argue. Ignoring a problem rarely makes it go away.

Second, even if this book were written by an individual with a disability, I would still face an important danger as the author. People with different kinds of disabilities have different concerns and different needs. Not all members of the disability community approach disability in the same way. Some parts of the Deaf community reject the label of disability altogether, despite deafness (and being hard of hearing more generally) regularly being classified as a disability. Something similar is found among individuals with autism. Autism Spectrum Disorder (ASD) is a broad diagnosis and covers a range of individuals. Some individuals on the spectrum, particularly those who are often referred to as "high functioning" or those who used to be diagnosed as having Asperger's syndrome, distance themselves from individuals on the spectrum who are nonverbal, or from those who are more seriously impaired. Even within the disability community, we sometimes find attitudes of "us versus them" or "we are not like them."

I want this book to undermine that attitude. Or at least chip away at it.

Chapters 2 and 3 focus on how we have inherited a long history of ableism and exclusion and how disability rights advocates secured important legal protections for people with disabilities. (Just as the term *racism* refers to behaviors or policies that discriminate against or devalue individuals on the basis of their race and the term *sexism* refers to behaviors or policies that discriminate against or devalue individuals on the basis of their sex, the term *ableism* refers to behaviors or policies that discriminate against or devalue people on the basis of disability.) Chapters 4 and 5 talk about how exclusion still happens in interpersonal and social ways, even though legal protections have been secured. While many kinds of physical barriers have been removed by legal protections, there are still plenty of social barriers to inclusion. The closing chapter, chapter 6, gives advice on how to begin changing our inherited culture, in which disability is still seen as something to be pitied, something to be avoided. There I argue that we all have a lot to learn about what it means to be human by valuing those who have disabilities.

In his book *I Am Strong*, mentioned above, Lamar Hardwick tells a story of growing up not realizing that he had ASD. But he did know that he was often excluded from his community. Church, where he should have found a sense of welcoming and belonging, would "only confirm what I already knew about myself. I was different. I was an outsider. I was a mystery that no one could figure out, and because I was so different and so deficient in my ability to relate well to others socially, it demanded that I be excluded from all attempts to build relationships with others, even God." But in the neighborhood candy store, he finally felt like he belonged. "The one thing that made me just like everyone else was the candy store. At the candy store, true community was present. Everyone was equal, and everyone was accepted, and although I can recall the beginning stages of discerning that I was different than the other kids, the candy store helped level the playing field."

My goal in the coming pages is to help us take steps to make our communities more like Hardwick's neighborhood candy store, where everyone is welcomed and valued. People who feel different, unvalued, and excluded tend to disappear from our lives. We have forcibly disappeared many with disabilities, through institutionalization, selective abortion, exclusion, discrimination, and ableism. But we have also made them so sufficiently unwelcome that they have withdrawn from our lives. And that makes us worse off, even if we understand why they might not want to persist in a community that doesn't properly value them.

Let's try to better understand individuals with disabilities. Let's own up to our cultural history of forcible exclusion. Let's learn to make our communities more inclusive and welcoming to those with disabilities. When we do these things, all of us will be better off.

The History
of Exclusion

2

There are parts of history that aren't pleasant to read. For instance, reading about the histories of slavery, racism, and sexism isn't something many people do for fun. And some people actively avoid such parts of history. They pretend these parts don't exist or need to be addressed because of their unpleasantness.

Much of the history covered in this chapter is like that. We don't like to think about this history. I suspect you won't like much of it and that parts of it will make you sad or angry. I think these reactions are not just understandable but appropriate. If reading about the history of exclusion and mistreatment of people because of their disabilities makes you sad or angry (or both), then I think your emotions are attuned to some important moral truths. We shouldn't be okay with the way people have been treated.

In reading what is to follow, many of you will want to say something like this: "But that wasn't *us*. We weren't involved. We don't do these things. And even if the treatment of individuals with disabilities isn't perfect, things are better now."

In one sense, I agree. There are a number of ways in which individuals with disabilities are treated less poorly now than they used to be. (I will talk about some of them in the coming pages of this book.) But these steps of progress were only brought about by those who directly confronted the previous history and worked to make things better.

In writing about dementia, Scottish theologian John Swinton uses the illustration of taking a flight to Boston. To get to where we want to be, we have to know where we are, where we are going, and the right way to get there from here. Swinton writes, "Understanding dementia is a bit like that. If we get on the wrong track or follow the wrong road map, we'll end up in the wrong place."

And while he is talking specifically about dementia, his advice is also true of disability in general. Part of getting things right is knowing where we are. But where we are depends on where we have been. The history matters. And we can learn from that history. Knowing how people made things better for individuals with disabilities in earlier parts of our history can help us see what we can do to continue to make our communities inclusive and inviting places.

HISTORY MATTERS

Some of you may still be wondering, "But why should I read this history, particularly given how unpleasant it is? Why can't I just jump into how to make my social environments and communities more inclusive?" I think there are at least three reasons not to jump ahead.

First, I think it is important to know this history because it is *our* history, even if it is not your personal history. This is a book about disability, exclusion, and the need for inclusion in the United States, and particularly about disability, exclusion, and the need for inclusion within Christian communities. So this history is the history of our country and of those who share our faith. If we had time, we would also look at other cultures, other countries, and other faith traditions. But that would be another book.

Second, we need to be honest about our collective past failures in order to better face our present challenges. A colleague of mine who writes on animal ethics wrote the following, which I think is also applicable here:

> We need honesty to meet the first challenge of facing up to some difficult facts about our daily choices that, in a less truthful mode, we might be tempted to rationalize away in order to preserve our personal comfort and convenience. But honesty alone is not enough, for simply facing the wider problems created by our daily food choices without resolving to be a part of their solutions is a recipe for "cognitive dissonance."

This book will make you aware of patterns of exclusion that you might not be aware of. We ought not simply deny or ignore this history in order to feel better about ourselves. We need to acknowledge that individuals with disabilities are still denied some of the same legal protections and rights that nondisabled individuals have. Honest acknowledgment is needed. But it is not enough. Once we know of these practices, we need to work to make our communities better in order to avoid our own cognitive dissonance.

Third, looking carefully at history can help us see important truths about our present culture. It is easier to see other people's failures and the assumptions that shaped their actions. But seeing others' failures and the assumptions they were based on can also help us question our own assumptions. If we are honest, we may find that we still share some of the assumptions that led to the problems we find in our own country and in the Church.

EXCLUSION IN THE CHURCH

Historically, Christian treatment of those with disabilities has been mixed. In parts of the Scriptures and writings of the Early Church, there is a close connection between disability, on the one hand, and sin, spiritual failure, and impurity, on the other. In Leviticus, individuals with physical disabilities weren't allowed to be priests because they were "defective" (21:16–24). Elisha punished the servant Gehazi with leprosy for his lack of faithfulness (2 Kings 5:20–27). This act associated disability and cultural exclusion with moral failing. Zechariah doubted Gabriel's promise of a child. As a result, the angel disabled him by striking him mute (Luke 1:8–20). Throughout the

Christian Scriptures, spiritual failure and deceit are regularly associated with blindness. Similarly, mental illness is linked with demonic possession. The cultural connection between disability, on the one hand, and impurity and sin, on the other, is very close. On one occasion, when Jesus's disciples encountered someone with a disability, they asked, "Who sinned? This man or his parents?" Jesus replied, "Neither" (John 9:1–3). In doing so, he broke this connection between disability and sin. But other parts of the New Testament still reinforce the belief that disability must be cured before the coming reign of God can be established.

For much of its history, the Church has reinforced this link between disability and moral or spiritual failing, especially sexual sin. Many Christians in the medieval period, for instance, endorsed the theory of maternal imagination. According to this theory, women who look at or think about inappropriate things during sex can cause their children to develop disabilities. The idea behind the theory goes back to the story of Jacob and Laban in the book of Genesis (chapter 30). Laban is Jacob's uncle and agrees that Jacob can marry his daughter Rachel in exchange for seven years of labor. But Laban tricks Jacob, marrying him to his other daughter, Leah, instead. Jacob then works another seven years to marry Rachel. A few years later, Jacob decides to return to the land of his forefathers, and Laban says he can take all the speckled or streaked sheep. So Jacob places striped markings on wooden rods by the sheep's watering trough so that when they see them, they will bear striped offspring. Similarly, it was thought that having sexually impure thoughts during conception could cause women to bear disabled offspring.

As Rebecca Chopp writes, "Most Christian traditions have equated disability with sin." During the medieval period in Europe, those with mental illnesses and disabilities, which were regularly attributed to demon possession or sin, were often imprisoned, sometimes tortured, or even executed. Even if they were tolerated within a community, they were seen as less valuable, as "lesser." Martin Luther, for example, referred to children with intellectual disabilities as "a mass of flesh with no soul who were 'filled with Satan,' the father of idiots." Leo X, who was pope from 1513 until his death in 1521, used individuals with disabilities as part of his dinner entertainment. Court jesters, who likely had intellectual disabilities, and Little People were demeaned for public amusement.

Now, this isn't to say that such attitudes were everywhere. During the same time, Christian monasteries and nunneries across Europe ran hospices for those with disabilities and mental illnesses. They found ways for them to be productive members of their local communities. Religious orders cared for individuals with disabilities as part of their larger mission to the sick, the poor, and the marginalized.

During the thirteenth and fourteenth centuries, disability was increasingly seen as a natural occurrence rather than as a spiritual lesson. Some theologians, like Albert the Great, thought that disability is part of the human condition. It is not, he insisted, a punishment for personal sin. Thomas Aquinas also saw disability as part of the human condition. He insisted that those with disabilities are human and not akin to irrational animals. Aquinas encouraged Dominican priests to give the sacrament of baptism to people with disabilities. At the same time, however, the Church often failed to love and care for individuals as it ought. (This failure wasn't limited to just those with disabilities.)

MORE RECENT EXCLUSION AND MISTREATMENT

With the Industrial Revolution, things in Europe generally became worse for individuals with disabilities since they weren't "productive" members of society. Families were less able to care for their members with disabilities given the changes to the economy and society. Conditions worsened, especially for those in urban areas, during the seventeenth, eighteenth, and nineteenth centuries as the economic pressures increased. Wealthy families often had the resources to keep children with disabilities at home and provide for them. Less wealthy families turned to institutions for their care. While the existence of such institutions might be seen as good, the conditions were far from it. A number of hospitals or asylums for children with disabilities had rates of death within the first year of a child's life of over 80%. It was common for individuals in these centuries to be kept in cells, which they might not ever leave. They were often naked or clothed only in rags, and they slept on the floor.

The history of the United States is also troubling, despite the close historical connection between the United States and Christianity. But there are some bright spots. The first code of laws among the European settlers in the Americas, *The Body of Liberties* adopted by the Massachusetts General Court in 1641, not only recognized individuals with disabilities but also excluded them from criminal punishment in many cases. In 1866, Edouard Seguin, an early American pioneer of special education, helped found the American Association on Mental Deficiency. It was the first association in the country devoted solely to the care and education of individuals with intellectual disabilities. Though it would take nearly fifty years before any state would require special education for individuals with cognitive impairments, there was clearly some concern about educating those individuals who had disabilities, both for their own good and for the good of the larger culture.

However, for much of its history, the US has used disability as a way of excluding individuals who were seen as a burden on the country. Laws often denied them access. The Immigration Acts of 1882 and 1924, for example, allowed government officials to restrict the immigration of those who were disabled or even likely to become so.

Individuals with intellectual impairment, epilepsy, and mental illness were specifically denied entrance into the US. Steamship companies that brought individuals with disabilities to ports of entry could be fined as much as $1,000 per offense. In the early twentieth century, immigration officials were told that "any mental abnormality whatever . . . justifies the statement that the alien is mentally defective," a judgment that could be used to prevent an individual's immigration into the US.

Perhaps not surprisingly, such laws resulted in a higher deportation rate for individuals from Asia than from Europe. Discrimination against individuals with disabilities often is closely connected with discrimination based on race. The history of IQ tests, for example, has racist overtones. Many individuals with disabilities already in the country were deported. In the late nineteenth century and the first few decades of the twentieth century, numerous cities—from San Francisco to Chicago—enacted laws that prohibited those with disabilities or other "mutilated or deformed bodies" from being out in public.

In the eighteenth century, many individuals with disabilities in the US were educated in small, community-based schools designed for this purpose. At the end of the nineteenth century, these smaller and more home-like facilities were gradually replaced by larger, often overcrowded, and usually greatly underfunded facilities that would both house and "educate" individuals with disabilities. Economies of scale and concerns over "ease of resident management" came to dominate, leading to larger facilities that basically amounted to warehousing individuals with disabilities. These facilities were often referred to as colonies. The number of individuals in such institutions increased by 50% between 1950 and 1970. It was widely recognized that the expanding populations in these facilities led to numerous problems. As one state-level administrator noted at the time, "As the worthy cases spill over into the corridors, the already inadequate personnel-to-resident ratios become impossible and there is little the staff can do except to fold laundry and keep a fire watch."

But little was done during much of the twentieth century to change these institutions until their levels of overcrowding, abuse, and dehumanization were brought to light. In 1966, Burton Blatt and Fred Kaplan published *Christmas in Purgatory: A Photographic Essay on Mental Retardation*, which documented the deplorable conditions at state institutions.

In 1972, investigative journalist Geraldo Rivera wrote an exposé, *Willowbrook: The Last Great Disgrace*, which focused on a state-supported institution for children with intellectual disabilities on Staten Island in New York. Willowbrook housed double the population it was designed for. Individuals slept on the hard floor, had rags for clothes, and were malnourished. Rivera's reporting contributed to a rising chorus of voices advocating for institutional reform. Willowbrook closed in 1987.

Overcrowded and abusive institutions were not the only problem in the US's treatment of individuals with disabilities. Many thought that individuals with disabilities, especially those with intellectual disabilities, should not reproduce. The state of Indiana first legalized the forced sterilization of individuals with disabilities in 1907. By 1912, eight states had similar laws. While the laws applied primarily to those with intellectual or developmental disabilities, individuals who were blind or deaf were also forcibly sterilized. Supreme Court Justice Oliver Wendell Holmes Jr. said in the decision of the *Buck v. Bell* case in 1927: "Three generations of imbeciles are enough." This decision upheld the forced sterilization of individuals with disabilities, and eventually more than thirty states engaged in such sterilizations. California's sterilization law, in particular, was part of the inspiration for Nazi eugenic practices. Forced sterilizations continued into at least the 1980s, resulting in over eighty thousand individuals with disabilities in the US being sterilized. In fact, such treatment is still legal in a number of states.

The use of disability as a way of marginalizing or discriminating was also closely connected with various forms of sexism and racism in the US. In the 1870s, influential educational leaders argued that attempts to educate women led to their becoming disabled. Disability was used to justify slavery in the nineteenth century. For instance, Samuel Cartwright, a medical doctor and proponent of scientific racism, argued that "blacks' physical and mental defects made it impossible for them to survive without white supervision and care." The term *mongoloid*, originally used to refer to individuals with Down syndrome, is rooted in anti-Asian racism. And as late as the 1940s, the claim that Native Americans were particularly prone to disability was used to justify withholding full rights to indigenous populations.

In the 1980s, the American Lutheran Church did not allow individuals with "'significant' physical or mental" disability to be ordained. These disabilities included multiple sclerosis, quadriplegia, and psychiatric disorders. Some major American seminaries did not admit students with disabilities because they worried those individuals would be unable to properly administer the sacraments.

CONCLUSION

As mentioned at the beginning of this chapter, the history of mistreatment of individuals with disabilities isn't pretty. There is a long history of equating disability with sin or moral failure. There is a long history of assuming that individuals with disabilities are less than fully human and not worthy of respect and value. There is a long history of thinking of disability primarily in economic terms. There is a long history of wanting to keep individuals with disabilities out of our communities and country. This history is important because similar attitudes persist far more than we would like to admit. These are all attitudes I have faced regarding our son. These are attitudes that led to the patterns of structural and interpersonal exclusion addressed at greater length in the next two chapters.

Structural
Exclusion

3

The previous chapter focused on ways in which our history shows a pattern of excluding and devaluing individuals with disabilities. In the past thirty years, the United States has taken steps toward inclusion. There have been important legal steps to protect individuals with disabilities from various kinds of discrimination. The history here is complex, and this short chapter can't do justice to the details. But I want to talk about the broad contours of the disability rights movement and three federal laws that it led to: Section 504 of the Rehabilitation Act of 1973, the Americans with Disabilities Act (ADA) in 1990, and the Individuals with Disabilities Education Act (IDEA) in 1990 (an updated version of the Education for All Handicapped Children Act of 1975). While these laws have helped secure *integration*, we will see in the next two chapters that they haven't achieved *inclusion*. Individuals with disabilities are still excluded in numerous ways despite the legal protections these laws have secured. And this is true at both interpersonal and structural levels. Just as this chapter makes the case for the need to remove physical barriers, the next will argue for the need to eliminate social barriers.

"TO DENY OR NOT TO DENY DISABILITY"

I begin this chapter with a story. It is not my story. Vic Finkelstein, himself disabled by a spinal cord injury, wrote a powerful piece entitled "To Deny or Not to Deny Disability." Finkelstein grew up in South Africa when it was divided by apartheid. He was imprisoned for his work to end apartheid and eventually fled to the United Kingdom. He saw firsthand the way that society can exclude and mistreat people simply on the basis of their race. Such exclusion hurt not only individual lives but also entire communities. And he saw something parallel with disability.

Finkelstein asks us to consider a village where all the residents are wheelchair users. It is a society built for those who have physical disabilities, namely mobility impairment. They have designed all the buildings to suit their physical needs. Doorways are only five feet tall; no ceiling is over seven feet four inches. Counters are low. Everyone lives a comfortable life in their wheelchair.

But then one day a group of able-bodied individuals comes to the village. The community is not designed for them. They are constantly banging their heads on the low door frames. They go to the doctors for care, but the doctors all use wheelchairs too. It doesn't dawn on the doctors to suggest raising the heights of the doorways. Instead, they prescribe helmets for the able-bodied visitors so they won't continue to get hurt when they bang their heads. They give them braces so they can walk hunched over and avoid banging their heads in the first place. Since workplaces weren't designed with upright employees in mind, those who don't use wheelchairs find it hard to get jobs.

And when they do get them, they find that their work environments get in the way of doing their jobs. Society is structured in a way that fails to consider their needs.

In this story, in which "the abled" and "the disabled" have switched roles, the script is flipped, so to speak. Finkelstein helps us see what our society looks and feels like to those who have disabilities. Our entire social lives are constructed for those who don't have disabilities. People with disabilities are discriminated against simply by the way our physical environments are structured without concern for those with disabilities.

The last paragraph of Finkelstein's parable is worth reproducing in whole:

One day, when the able-bodied were sitting together and discussing their problems they realised that they were never consulted by the wheelchair-users about this in the little society. In fact they realised that there may be solutions to their problems which had never occurred to the wheelchair users simply because they never looked at these in the same way as those who had them. It occurred to these able-bodied disabled people that perhaps the cause of their problems had a social solution—they suggested that the door and ceiling heights be changed! They formed a union to fight segregation. Of course some of the wheelchair-users thought the able-bodied disabled were failing to accept and adjust to their disabilities, and they had chips on their shoulders because they argued so strongly for social change and a change in attitudes by the wheelchair-users. The able-bodied disabled even argued that perhaps, just perhaps, their disabilities could be overcome (and disappear!) with changes in society.

Finkelstein's story illustrates what is now often referred to as the social model of disability. At its core, the social model suggests that disability isn't primarily a function of individuals and their bodies. Rather, disability is primarily about a mismatch between bodies with impairments and the ways their larger social environment is structured. The social model is sometimes summarized in the slogan "disabled by society not by our bodies." (The social model is often contrasted with the medical model, which I discuss later in chapter 5.)

THE DISABILITY RIGHTS MOVEMENT

The social model played a central role in the disability rights movement in the second half of the twentieth century. It led to a reexamination of the need to accommodate people with disabilities in the ways our communities and society are structured. This movement in turn led to a number of legal developments that sought to make the US a more hospitable and welcoming place for those with disabilities.

The disability rights movement doesn't have a clear beginning. Groups in Illinois and California began working in the early 1960s on ways for people with disabilities to live independently rather than in group homes or care facilities. It was spurred on by the 1964 passage of the Civil Rights Act. Other legislation gave individuals with disabilities some legal protections: the establishment of Medicare and Medicaid in 1965, the Architectural Barriers and Fair Housing Acts in 1968, Title IX of the Education Amendments Act in 1972. Some of this legislation wasn't primarily about disability. But it did provide more protection of civil rights. And even those, like Title IX, that didn't specifically mention disability became part of what motivated the disability rights movement.

As with black pride and gay pride movements, from which they drew inspiration, people with disabilities sought to affirm their disabilities as positive parts of their identities. They realized that achieving equal rights would be difficult if the dominant narrative was still that disability was always and only a bad thing. They wanted to change this narrative, to affirm the value of their lives and experiences. But they also realized that they would need to secure legal protections as part of this larger cultural movement.

Hubert Humphrey, who helped write the 1964 Civil Rights Act, began work to amend it to include disability in 1972. But politicians, including leading African Americans, opposed the change. They were afraid that doing so would "dilute" the Civil Rights Act.

THE FIRST FEDERAL LEGAL PROTECTIONS

The Rehabilitation Act of 1973 aimed to shift federal assistance away from mere vocational rehabilitation and toward the overall lives of individuals with disabilities. Prior to its passage, a staffer—whose identity seems to be lost to history—inserted forty-six words that changed the legal protections of individuals with disabilities in the US. These words are from Section 504:

> No otherwise qualified handicapped individual in the United States as defined in Section 7(6), shall, solely by reason of his handicap, be excluded from the participation in, be denied the benefits of, or be subject to discrimination under any program or activity receiving Federal financial assistance.

The language here was based directly on previously existing civil rights legislation. Section 504 sought to extend certain civil rights protections directly to disability and was the first comprehensive civil rights law in the US for people with disabilities. But it was limited only to programs receiving federal tax dollars. Nevertheless, it was a beginning.

Disability activists, however, saw the need to provide direct and all-encompassing protections from discrimination against those with disabilities. What they wanted was federal legislation that would give the same range of civil rights protections to people with disabilities that other

Americans had. Why should someone be denied access to a restaurant or a movie theater simply because they had epilepsy? Similar discrimination based on race had been outlawed more than twenty years earlier. The first national organization advocating for disability as a whole, rather than for a specific disability, was the American Coalition of Citizens with Disabilities, an organization started in 1974. They began holding rallies across the country that brought disability to the public awareness. In 1977, approximately 150 activists organized by the ACCD occupied a federal building in San Francisco, protesting that the protections promised by Section 504 hadn't materialized. They did not leave until the secretary of the Department of Health, Education, and Welfare finally signed the regulations twenty-five days later.

Protections for individuals with disabilities slowly increased over the course of the next decade. But in the mid 1980s, a number of legal cases began to narrow the protections of Section 504. Under the leadership of President Ronald Reagan, both the White House and Congress sought to limit disability-based protections. Reagan wanted to weaken Section 504 and the Education for All Handicapped Children Act (more on this law in a bit). By doing so, he hoped to eventually undermine the Civil Rights Act.

In 1981, Evan J. Kemp Jr. wrote an op-ed to the *New York Times* titled "Aiding the Disabled: No Pity, Please." In it, Kemp criticized Jerry Lewis and the Muscular

Dystrophy Association for reinforcing stigma against individuals with disabilities:

> With its emphasis on "poster children" and "Jerry's kids," the telethon focuses primarily on children. The innocence of children makes them ideal for use in a pity appeal. But by celebrating disabled children and ignoring disabled adults, it seems to proclaim that the only socially acceptable status for disabled people is their early childhood. The handicapped child is appealing and huggable—the adolescent or mature adult is a cripple to be avoided.

Kemp, like other disability rights activists, opposed both the infantilization of individuals with disabilities and the way the telethon suggested that disability means helplessness. Both of these reinforced pity as the primary social response to disability. According to these activists, what was needed wasn't pity. It was legal protections.

THE ADA

In the mid 1980s, a number of both Republicans and Democrats—almost all of whom had a direct connection to individuals with disabilities, either themselves or family members—worked to write such a law. Their goal was a comprehensive law requiring equal opportunity for people with disabilities. They hoped to pass it in 1986. They were lucky to get it passed four years later in the face of significant opposition.

In 1990, the Americans with Disabilities Act (ADA) was signed into law. It was the largest signing ceremony in the Rose Garden to date and the first time in US history that such an event began with a religious prayer. Senator Ted Kennedy referred to the ADA as "the Emancipation Proclamation for Persons with Disabilities." It extended protections against discrimination on the basis of disability in the private and the public sectors. No longer could people be legally denied employment, the use of public transportation, or access to various public goods and services simply because they had a disability. It wasn't until this act—in 1990—that citizens with disabilities had the full range of civil rights that nondisabled citizens had. Churches and other religious bodies lobbied to be excluded from its requirements; this change was accepted as a last minute concession. Section 12187 of the ADA specifies that "religious organizations or entities controlled by religious organizations, including places of worship" are exempt from having to follow the ADA.

We don't even notice many of the changes brought about by the ADA because they have become part of our lives. People in wheelchairs aren't the only ones who benefit from curb cutouts. Parents pushing strollers and cyclists do too. Closed captioning, originally developed for those with hearing impairments, lets me watch Netflix in bed without bothering my sleeping wife.

The ADA was a good step. It would become the template for similar legislation around the world, including the UN's Convention on the Rights of Persons with Disabilities. (Interestingly, the US is not among the 159 nations that have ratified this convention, despite its being based on US law.) But for all their influence worldwide, there is evidence that these acts haven't done everything they need to and are not uniformly followed. For instance, workers who have disabilities are more likely to lose their positions during downturns of economic markets. And even now, in the US individuals with at least one disability are over twice as likely to be poor.

And think of the exemption that churches and religious groups won. They actively campaigned to not have to follow the ADA. And they succeeded. What if, rather than seeking to be excluded from these requirements, churches saw them as a bare minimum and actively sought to exceed them? What if churches instead were beacons of inclusion that set a high standard for what inclusive and welcoming communities ought to look like? (More on this in chapter 6.)

PUBLIC EDUCATION FOR CHILDREN WITH DISABILITIES

Public education for people with disabilities has lagged behind laws that prevent racial discrimination. Even when the US Supreme Court ended "separate but equal" public education in 1954, students with disabilities were often kept out of public schools. When they were given access to public education, they were often educated in a segregated way that achieved (and perhaps aimed at) lower educational quality. The importance of the *Brown v. Board of Education* decision for students with disabilities and their right to a public education didn't fully develop for another two decades. It was not until 1972 that the *Mills v. Board of Education of the District of Columbia* decision extended the right to a public education to children with disabilities. The decision also established the principle that lack of educational funding cannot be used to deny public education to students with disabilities.

When the Education for All Handicapped Children Act (EAHCA) was passed in 1975, one in eight children with a disability was completely excluded from public education. And of those who did attend public school, over half received no accommodations for their disabilities.

When the EAHCA's regulations were implemented in 1977, all students, regardless of disability, were given the right to a "free appropriate public education" (FAPE). Updated in 1990, the EAHCA became the Individuals with Disabilities Education Act (IDEA). IDEA requires not only that schools provide a FAPE, but also that it be done in the "least restrictive environment" (LRE). That is, education must be offered in a way that, as with other kinds of inclusion and integration, actively works to undermine the "separate but equal" approach to public education that has marked much of US history. According to IDEA:

each public agency must ensure that: (i) to the maximum extent appropriate, children with disabilities, including children in public or private institutions or other care facilities, are educated with children who are nondisabled; and (ii) special classes, separate schooling, or other removal of children with disabilities from the regular educational environment occurs only if the nature or severity of the disability is such that education in regular classes with the use of supplementary aids and services cannot be achieved satisfactorily.

Since public education is administered in the US at the state rather than the federal level, each state develops its own application of IDEA. Each state also determines its own level and method of funding special education in public schools. The failure to properly fund special education puts pressures on public schools and districts that contribute to their often adversarial relationships with parents—particularly given that IDEA is an "unfunded mandate" for state departments of education. And this is why, as I shared in chapter 1, families have to advocate to make sure their children with disabilities receive the public education they are promised. Even systems made to protect individuals with disabilities often cause hardship.

Interpersonal Exclusion

4

Chapter 4 begins with good news: you are halfway done reading this book! Feel free to take a short break. Have an espresso or two. Perhaps a glass of wine. Put your feet up. It's downhill from here.

Before moving into new terrain, here is a brief recap. Chapter 2 recounted some of the history of excluding and devaluing individuals with disabilities, both in the United States and in the Church. Much of that material was depressing. Chapter 3 sought to show how things have gotten better. Through the disability rights movement and resulting legislation, various legal protections have been secured for individuals with disabilities. Things improved for people with disabilities in the US substantially in the 1970s, 1980s, and early 1990s.

These improvements certainly weren't uniform. And as my family's own story in chapter 1 shows, laws are often not followed. A free appropriate public education (FAPE), while promised to all students with disabilities in the US, isn't always given. Even though the Americans with Disabilities Act (ADA) has been federal law since 1990, it too isn't always followed. Over the past year, I have let over a dozen local businesses in my community know that their parking lots are in violation of the ADA. A number of them have responded well and sought to correct the problem quickly. Others have been more hesitant. I have reported several to the Department of Justice's Civil Rights Division, which is the prescribed means for securing ADA compliance. At the time of this writing, over a year has passed since I first pointed out to a local coffee shop that they are in violation of the ADA. The owner has denied it, stalled, and even tried to get me in trouble with my employer for asking that he follow the law.

This resistance is widespread. Title III of the ADA addresses accessibility of public accommodations such as restaurants, movie theaters, and schools. Nationwide, over 6,600 ADA Title III lawsuits were filed in 2016, an increase of 60% from the previous year.

So the legal protections are clearly not sufficient to secure that individuals with disabilities have equal access in society. Furthermore, in the present contentious political climate, these protections are at risk. In the first year of the Trump presidency, for instance, the House Judiciary Committee advanced legislation that, if passed, would make enforcing the current protections afforded by the ADA more difficult. In the *Washington Post*, Lennard Davis and David Perry recently wrote that this legislation, misleadingly called the ADA Education and Reform Act, aims neither at education nor at reform. Instead it would, in essence, make the ADA optional since it would make enforcement of it significantly harder. So far, fortunately, it hasn't passed. If this law were to pass, I wouldn't be able to file ADA violation complaints with the Department of Justice, since I myself am not disabled. The law would thus transfer the work of ensuring compliance to the disability community, burdening the community that the ADA sought to protect. We can't assume that the current legal protections will remain in place in the future.

But in this chapter, I want to set aside these structural issues. For now, suppose that the picture I have been painting of the present situation is wrong. I want you to assume that the legal protections of the ADA and IDEA are uniformly followed. Assume that these laws aren't under threat. Assume that there is no formal or legal exclusion of individuals with disabilities from their communities or from public goods. In other words, assume that individuals with disabilities have achieved full integration into their communities.

But being in a physical space and having various legal protections do not mean that one is fully a part of that community. Many immigrants' experiences bear this out. Integration is not the same as inclusion. As I am using the term *inclusion*, it requires more than just legal protections and physical presence. Inclusion requires full opportunity for participation and value in one's community. Many local sports leagues, for instance, don't forbid individuals with disabilities from playing. They don't have to because they indicate in other ways that people with disabilities are not expected. Perhaps not wanted. Think about it for a minute: is your local soccer or lacrosse league structured in a way that makes individuals with disabilities feel welcome or valued?

It is especially here, at the level of inclusion, that I think we need to continue to work, continue to fight, continue to advocate. This chapter focuses on what I will refer to as social barriers or moments of exclusion—ways that our communities exclude rather than include that are often unnoticed by, and perhaps are even unnoticeable to, those who aren't close to them. I can't, in one chapter, deal with the full range of moments of exclusion. I will address two in particular: language and time. I hope these are enough to show just how widespread interpersonal exclusion often is.

LANGUAGE

At the 2009 Special Olympics World Winter Games, the "Spread the Word to End the Word" campaign was launched. Initiated by two college students, Souren Palumbo and Tim Shriver, the campaign sought to "promote the positive contributions people with intellectual disabilities make to communities around the world combined with a simple call to action that also symbolizes positive attitude change and a commitment to make the world a more accepting place for all people." In particular, the word it wanted to end is *retard*.

"Retarded" is often used as a slur, as are other words that have their origin in classifying people with disabilities. The exact functioning of slurs is contested among linguists. In general, they are used to target and denigrate an entire class of individuals. They are used to make those people they refer to feel like they are unwelcome or somehow "other." Their derogatory content is a function of various social factors. Many slurs are racial or ethnic in nature. Others focus on sex, gender, religion, immigration status, or nationality.

Calling a person with a disability "a retard" functions to portray them as less valuable. And the same is true of words such as *idiot*, *moron*, and *imbecile*. Many of these terms began as classifications for degrees of intellectual disability. Such a label was used to deny people a public education, institutionalize them, or allow the state to forcibly sterilize them. These words have a long history of being used to harm people with disabilities. Even if a term wasn't initially used in a derogatory way, language changes. Words can come to be understood as problematic even if they were earlier accepted. Both *colored* and *negro* function in a similar way. Calling a person with an intellectual disability "a retard" or "an imbecile" functions to devalue them.

Often these words are used as a slur not only against those who are disabled, but also against others. In these cases, the slur is used to lump its target in with those who do have the disability. Calling a person "a retard," even if they don't have an intellectual disability, is a way of devaluing them. That is the point of using the word as an insult.

Consider uses such as "that's retarded" to refer to something the speaker doesn't like. Or when "she's such a spaz" refers to someone who is clumsy. Or "that's crazy" to refer to something that is difficult to believe or unexpected. As with its primary use against the group the slur picks out, offense or ill will need not be intended for its use to be problematic.

Our language shapes our thinking in ways that aren't always obvious to us. Language carries meaning and association beyond dictionary definitions. Think, for instance, of how often "blind" and "deaf" are used in religious contexts to refer to sinfulness or guilt or disobedience. Unfortunately, many of these issues are made more complex by the fact that the Bible uses these metaphors. The Gospel of John, for instance, is particularly vivid in how it associates blindness with sin. Just because the metaphor is biblical doesn't mean it is not problematic. Biblical language often reflects the cultural assumptions in which it was written. And we can distance ourselves from those assumptions, especially if they are problematic, while still respecting the Scriptures. Most Christians have rejected the cosmological assumptions behind the Scriptural passages describing the world as flat with four corners. So too we can reject some of the ableist assumptions that Scripture seems to employ even while celebrating its central message of liberation for the oppressed and marginalized. If a church realized that some of the language it uses in songs or liturgy might be exclusionary, it could work to become more welcoming.

As with derogatory language rooted in sexual orientation such as "queer," some people with disabilities have sought to take these slurs and turn them into a badge of honor. A friend of mine who has a mobility impairment, for instance, sometimes sports a t-shirt that proclaims "Proud Crip." This process is called reclaiming and plays an important role in Gay Pride and Disability Pride movements. But those who don't share these identities ought not use these reclaimed terms.

In addition to slurs, language can also be problematic in other ways. Suppose you meet someone who has a disability. Asking "what's your condition?" is better than asking "what's wrong with you?" The former focuses on a disability to be dealt with. The latter suggests the primary problem is something about the person that needs to be fixed. But even better than asking "what"—which tends to put a diagnosis before the person—is asking "why" questions. Why do you use a cane? Why do you find it hard to open that door? Language matters.

While talking about language, it is also important to contrast person-first and identity-first language. Notice that in chapter 1 I always referred to "my son with a disability," not "my disabled son." "Person with a disability" is an instance of person-first language. It is a way of focusing on a person's humanity and individuality rather than leading with their disability. As theologian John Swinton says, using person-first language puts the "focus on the person as opposed to the label." Many people with disabilities think person-first language is preferable to identity-first language. It is a good default we should work to foster.

In the previous paragraph, I said many people with disabilities prefer person-first language. I said *many* for a reason. As with other issues, the disability community isn't uniform with regard to person-first versus identity-first language. Many Deaf individuals, for whom their deafness is part of their culture and language, prefer to be called Deaf rather than "a person with a hearing impairment." (The capital *D* in "Deaf," as opposed to "deaf," signals their cultural identity and not just an auditory disability. Many members of the Deaf community don't think their Deafness is a disability. If this is correct, then they may not be afforded the legal protections discussed in chapter 3.) Many people with an autism diagnosis prefer to be called "autistic" rather than "a person with autism," given how they see their autism as part of their identity. Many autistics are proud of their autism and see it as a form of neurodiversity rather than a disability. And some scholars oppose person-first language because they think it hides how people are disabled by society.

The issues surrounding group identity and language use are complex. It is best to use the language that people prefer as an act of hospitality. Until you know an individual's personal preference, defaulting to person-first language is a good general practice. But listen to what they ask you to use. Making people feel welcome and valued by our language is better than making them feel excluded, even if we don't mean to. Better than simply using hospitable language, though, is actually entering into a sustained, deepening relationship with a person who has a disability. Person-first language is good; person-first relationships are better.

TIME

Another way that our communities are not welcoming to those with disabilities involves time. This is particularly true given the frantic pace that governs our modern lives. It is a pace that is often exclusionary of individuals and families with disabilities, for a number of reasons. Let me highlight two.

Certain tasks simply take longer for individuals with disabilities to accomplish. I had a good friend, Ray, who had a profound stutter. (Unfortunately, Ray died a number of years ago.) While he had always stuttered, it got significantly worse as his Parkinson's progressed in his later years. Conversations with Ray often took three or four times longer because he would get stuck on words or couldn't get his sentences out. It was clear on Ray's face just how frustrating this was to him. But it was just as visible to me—and surely to him—the frustration and discomfort that others felt. Their faces often showed that taking the time to have deep and meaningful conversations with him just wasn't worth their time or energy. Over the years, I watched him start to say less, to verbally withdraw. While he was still physically welcome, he was relegated to being an observer rather than a participant in social interactions.

Here is another example. Our son's disabilities impact his gross motor skills. He was delayed in walking and couldn't run before the age of nine. I mentioned in chapter 1 that when we lived in Idaho, our family used to regularly go trick-or-treating in our neighborhood with a number of other families. Now, all these families cared about our son. They were not strangers. They were families who were invested in our family. We had an especially large group the Halloween when Jameson was five. There were probably about fifteen kids, and close to that many parents. Some of the kids were older than Jameson and some were younger. When it came time to start walking from house to house to collect the night's candy, as I mentioned in chapter 1, within a few minutes Jameson was already falling behind. He simply couldn't keep up given his difficulty walking. I am sure the other kids didn't give it a thought as they rushed to fill their bags with the night's haul. Perhaps the other parents didn't notice either, or perhaps they simply needed to keep up with their kids, as my wife needed to keep up with our daughter.

But my friend Stephen noticed. He and one of his boys walked the slow walk with us. They gave us the gifts of time and companionship so we didn't have to be on our own as we went about the fairly typical task of asking complete strangers for free candy. Being with us mattered more to them than hitting every house. I don't think I will ever forget that night and the way in which something as simple as taking the extra time to walk slower showed that Jameson mattered to them.

Theologian John Swinton uses the phrase "malignant social psychology" to refer to episodes like these. By malignant social psychology, Swinton means social interactions that happen in such a way as to diminish the value of certain people for the convenience or preference of others. Moments of exclusion are episodes of malignant social psychology. Swinton gives the example of how people often talk *about* a person with disabilities, as if they weren't there, instead of *to* those individuals. How we often don't take the additional time that some disabilities require is another example.

These malignant interactions often aren't done out of malice. They are often done carelessly or thoughtlessly. We often don't even notice that we have done them. Nobody tried to exclude Jameson on Halloween. It just happened. As seen earlier in the discussion of language, moments of exclusion don't have to be intentional to be problematic. As also was the case with Ray and his stutter, some individuals with certain forms of autism have difficultly engaging in conversations that change topics or directions too quickly. Unless we are careful, they can be left out of conversations, even if no one intends to exclude them. Over time, again like Ray, these individuals can start to engage less with others. (In the next chapter, I talk about some related interpersonal struggles that can happen.)

Valuing people means taking the time to be truly present with them. Just as inclusion requires more than just being *in* a particular space, being present requires more than just being *near* someone for a short time. It requires slowing down and investing in the lives of those around us.

CONCLUSION

As I said earlier, these two examples of moments of exclusion aren't intended to be exhaustive. Other moments of exclusion can pop up in almost any environment. The music at church may be too loud for those with sensory processing issues. Figurative language can be difficult for some autistic individuals to follow. Sports leagues, community events, or church vacation bible schools may prevent some with disabilities from participating, based on how they are run.

Inclusive environments are about providing acceptance and support that people need. Not every event or place can be made accessible to everyone, in part because sometimes an accommodation for one person, such as a service dog, may be problematic for another, such as a person with severe allergies. But making our environments more inclusive is important. One of the first steps is to realize that we need to change some of our social dynamics. We need to listen to those who have disabilities when they tell us what we can do to improve. But it is difficult to listen to those who aren't in our lives.

Some people's disabilities may not even be noticeable to us, particularly if we are not paying attention. My friend Carlyle was once told that he couldn't be disabled since he rides a Harley, despite the fact that he is autistic and has a paralyzed arm. Similarly, we may not notice a friend's disabling depression if we are too focused on other things or if they feel they can't trust us.

As I said earlier, it's not enough for us to remove physical barriers that prevent people with disabilities from being in our environments. Don't get me wrong; removing these physical barriers is important. But doing so is not the whole of what we need to do. We have to do more. Social barriers can often be more exclusionary than physical barriers, in part because they are harder for many of us to notice. Removing these social barriers, these moments of exclusion, is part of working toward true inclusion.

Social
Challenges

5

The previous chapter dealt with moments of exclusion that people with disabilities often face. This chapter deals with some of the many social challenges that arise from disabilities. These challenges are not unrelated to the need to eliminate moments of exclusion. And, as in the previous chapter, the examples here are not intended to be exhaustive. They are just a sample of the many ways in which disability can affect our social lives. I will not address lack of adequate college opportunities for individuals with intellectual disabilities and autism. I won't talk about the challenge for ongoing caregiving that some disabilities require. But all of these challenges, both those I address and those I pass over, negatively affect individuals and their families. They also negatively affect the life we live together. As a result, all of us will be better off if we make our communities more inclusive and supportive.

Part of caring about a person is caring about what they care about. If we care about people with disabilities, and care about including them, we will care about the challenges they face. Knowing how we can help address these challenges requires that we think about them. As with our history, we need to be honest about the present if we are to work toward a better and more inclusive future.

FINANCIAL REALITIES

When many people think about disability, they don't consider the way it impacts families financially. But disability often does involve financial difficulty. Individuals who acquire disabilities, perhaps through a spinal cord injury or a traumatic brain injury, are significantly more likely to declare bankruptcy. Even apart from bankruptcy, disability is often financially taxing. Regular developmental, speech, occupational, or physical therapies may be required. Some disabilities involve medical complications that require surgery or medication. Such treatment is often expensive and not always covered by insurance. Furthermore, those who have disabilities are both less likely to work and usually make less money even when they do work. Here are a few statistics that I hope will give you a sense of how large these problems are.

The 2016 Disability Statistics Annual Report indicates that adults with disabilities are less than half as likely to be employed. And that gap is widening. In fact, the unemployment rate for people with disabilities is presently higher than it was in 1990 when the Americans with Disabilities Act was passed. Over one in five individuals with disabilities in the US live in poverty, significantly over the national poverty rate of 13.8%. Companies such as Goodwill, which is one of the largest employers of people with disabilities in the country, usually pay workers with disabilities markedly less than the federal minimum wage. This is legal thanks to a provision of the Fair Labor Standard Act.

According to the Census Bureau, the median earnings for individuals sixteen years old or older with disabilities are less than 70% of the average income for able-bodied workers. (These figures don't include those adults with disabilities who are institutionalized. So the numbers are even more stark than this statistic suggests.)

The pay gap for women with disabilities is greater than for men with disabilities. This illustrates *intersectionality*, a term coined by civil rights advocate and law professor Kimberlé Crenshaw. Intersectionality points to where different social categories such as race, class, or disability status can create overlapping and interdependent systems of discrimination or disadvantage. Black women sometimes face discrimination that neither white women nor black men face. In similar fashion, individuals with disabilities who are women, racial minorities, or members of the LGBTQ community often face additional struggles that white men with disabilities do not face. There is reason to think, for instance, that autism is underdiagnosed in females because it often looks different for them than it does for males. Given that the diagnostic tests for autism were created with males in mind, this shouldn't be surprising.

Similarly, individuals with disabilities in the US are more likely to live in the South. This correlates both with higher levels of poverty and with a greater percentage of the population who is African American. Intersectionality strikes again.

Awareness of these issues, along with an appreciation for her art, led me to commission a painting by artist Sevy Marie for the cover of this book. It is a gripping painting, and I love that she titled it "Dancing with Jameson." But I am also aware that since Sevy is nonverbal, her opportunities for employment are greatly reduced, even if they shouldn't be. This perhaps small gesture of commissioning the painting is just one concrete way to support the work, art, and lives of people with disabilities.

Financial pressures and concerns about burdening one's family are often greatest at the end of life. These concerns affect people's choices about their own care. They illustrate the social pressures that shape our lives together. Those with sufficient financial means, for instance, are significantly less likely to seek assisted suicide when they become disabled than are people who are poor. The likelihood of having a disability also increases substantially with age. While fewer than 1% of children five years old or younger in the US have a disability, over 35% of individuals over the age of sixty-five do. Those of us who have not yet been personally affected by disability are likely to be in the future. We will feel the financial pressure.

Many of us haven't given much thought to the financial issues related to disability. We are fortunate we can avoid these issues, since they don't personally affect us. But one of the unfortunate consequences of how our culture has hidden disability from our lives is the resulting ignorance. We are often ignorant of things that don't directly affect us. Sometimes we are even ignorant of what affects those we care about. Learning about these issues can help us be better friends, better family members, to those who do face them. Learning about these issues can help us be better citizens and better Christians.

We are ignorant not just about finances and employment. Other forms of ignorance lead to other social pressures that we need to address. For instance, research shows that inclusive education is good for those students who lack disabilities as well as for those who have them. But ignorance about this research leads to our schools being needlessly segregated. Ignorance makes parents of children without disabilities think they don't need to know about special education in their schools. Ignorance makes students learning to be teachers think that classes on special education are optional for their career path. Ignorance makes those studying for the ministry think they don't need classes on the theology of disability. They can't imagine that they will have to address disability in their churches one day.

HEALTH CARE BIAS AGAINST DISABILITY

Ignorance and bias extend into the health care field as well. Expecting parents are ignorant about the lives of individuals with disabilities. They fear what disability means. This fear is one of the main reasons expecting parents seek prenatal screening. These screenings include tests such as amniocentesis, chorionic villus sampling (CVS), and maternal blood serum tests. These tests screen for disabilities such as cleft lip and palate, Down syndrome (also known as trisomy 21), spina bifida, and other neural tube abnormalities. These tests can certainly be useful. It would have been good to know prior to Allison's going into labor that our son might require a pacemaker immediately upon birth. (Fortunately, he didn't need one.)

But the information we get from prenatal diagnoses isn't neutral. Having information can pressure us, sometimes subtly, to act in certain ways. Prenatal cleft lip diagnoses, for instance, are one of the leading reasons for abortion in the United Kingdom. But most cleft lips can be restored through surgery. According to the British National Health Service, there was a 92% termination rate for positive prenatal Down syndrome diagnoses in the UK between 1989 and 1995 when the Disability Discrimination Act (DDA), the UK law similar to the ADA, was passed. You might think that this number would have decreased after individuals with disabilities secured legal protections under the DDA and ADA. However, abortion rates for prenatal diagnoses of Down syndrome have actually increased in the US since the ADA's passage in 1990.

Negative attitudes about disabilities appear to be structured into the training some young health care workers receive. In 2015, college students studying nursing and other health professions were surveyed. The results were startling. 62% thought an autism diagnosis would be sufficient reason to terminate their own pregnancy. 63% would pursue abortion for a prenatal Down syndrome diagnosis. 69% thought that fetuses with small congenital disorders, such as the lack of a finger, should be aborted. 57% indicated that children with disabilities such as Down syndrome or autism don't enrich society. (Interestingly, those surveyed who self-identified as Jewish were more likely to favor abortion than those who self-identified as

Arab. This may catch us off guard, given that this practice is arguably a form of eugenics. And it is estimated that over six million Jews were killed for eugenic reasons during the Holocaust.) The researchers suggested that these attitudes could impact quality of care or advice medical professionals give to families affected by disability.

Adults with disabilities may face another challenge from health care professionals. Many people still think that people with disabilities should not become pregnant or be parents. In fact, some parents with disabilities are deemed unfit by the state, resulting in their children being removed from their custody.

Individuals with disabilities are at risk for receiving inferior health care treatment based on these negative attitudes. Doctors, assuming that a health concern is related to disability, may not actively seek another cause. In this way, the doctor sees the disability rather than the person. And as discussed in chapter 4, the doctor may rush through an appointment, not recognizing the additional time a person with disabilities needs. Doctors and nurses are on tight schedules, after all.

Furthermore, there is a danger that medical professionals will think the primary problem with disability is a medical issue that needs to be treated or cured. They may fail to see that many of the difficulties faced by those with disabilities are actually social in nature. They may fail to take seriously a person's experience and input on their own care.

OVERLY MEDICALIZING DISABILITY

It is tempting for both laypeople and health care professionals to think of disabilities as medical issues to be fixed. Disability is then primarily seen as an issue of bodies in need of repair, perhaps even a cure. This is what is often referred to as the medical model of disability. We ought to reject this approach to disability in general. The medical model should not be the primary lens through which we understand disability.

Don't get me wrong. Some disabilities do involve medical challenges. Many of the individuals with our son's condition have problems with their heart valves. A number of them are prone to kidney cysts. Some need feeding tubes. All of these are medical issues caused by the underlying disability.

The lives of many people with disabilities have drastically improved due to advances in medical care. Insulin and diabetes research in the 1920s led to a significant increase in life expectancy for people with diabetes. There have been major improvements in care and treatment for spinal cord injuries in the past forty years. Millions of individuals worldwide develop acquired disabilities through preventable diseases such as malaria or TB. Working to eliminate these conditions decreases the number of people disabled by them. We ought to work toward reducing conditions that cause disabilities. But doing so doesn't mean we shouldn't also work to change social and structural issues faced by those who have disabilities.

The advance of medical technology and testing can make it easier for us to see disability primarily through a medical lens. This encourages us to think disability needs to be cured, to be fixed. As useful as medical technology is, it can be problematic in how it shapes our thinking. When we think of disability as primarily a medical issue, it is too easy to overlook the social and political injustices, such as those discussed in chapters 2, 3, and 4, that people with disabilities face.

Medicine's power over our collective imagination is powerful. It can shape our values, even if we don't notice that influence. Modern medicine is important, but it becomes problematic when it becomes the primary way we understand the human experience. Just as Jameson is more than his initial diagnosis, people with disabilities are more than what modern medicine says about their conditions. Too often a medical lens reduces people to their disabilities. And when we use this lens, we run the risk of losing their humanity. And our own.

INTERPERSONAL CHALLENGES

Being friends with people who are different from us is sometimes difficult. But just because it is difficult doesn't mean it is not important. People with disabilities need friends just like the rest of us. But research and personal experience both indicate that disabilities have an effect on friendships, both in terms of quality and number.

Jean Vanier founded the L'Arche communities, where people with disabilities and those without live in community with one another. He is all too familiar with exclusion individuals with disabilities or mental illness face in social settings. "The shared pain and the place of meeting between people with mental illnesses and people with intellectual disabilities is the collective experience of being rejected and often despised; of being seen as different or mad, foolish or crazy."

Too often a person with a disability is primarily seen through the lens of their disability. Even their caregivers, teachers, or medical staff can focus on their disability and fail to affirm their full humanity. The disability becomes all that another can see. Individuals with disabilities often also find that others see them as broken or needing to be fixed or cured. They become their diagnostic label rather than a human being who shares hopes, fears, feelings, and experiences just as others do.

We sometimes infantilize or diminish the agency of those who have disabilities. I have noticed that when I push my father-in-law in his wheelchair, the waitstaff at restaurants sometimes ask me what he would like to eat. Simply because of the wheelchair, they assume he needs me to order for him. In his book *The Enabled Life*, Roy McCloughry tells the story of a woman in a wheelchair. She was used to people addressing the person pushing her wheelchair rather than her—that is, until she broke a leg. Now that it looked as if her disability was temporary rather than permanent, suddenly people treated her differently, as if she was a real person.

Disability is often reduced to a stereotype. We assume that the person who uses a wheelchair doesn't have an interest in sports. We assume that the person with a hearing aid might also have an intellectual disability because they didn't understand what we said. We don't imagine that the problem was the background noise that we ourselves didn't notice. We assume that people with autism aren't interested in social interaction or being invited out with friends. We think that autistic individuals are loners or introverts. But research suggests that many people with autism want more social interaction and more friends than they currently have. Many of their behaviors that give the impression of a lack of social interest are caused by their autism. But they desire social interaction and friendship just like all humans do.

Consider, for instance, eye contact. Failure to make eye contact is sometimes taken to indicate a lack of interest. Or it just might make us uncomfortable. But many people with autism find it difficult to pay attention to conversations while looking at people's faces. Their lack of eye contact is actually a way for them to try to be engaged. But this runs contrary to the expectations and preferences of those of us who don't have autism. We make those with autism play by our social interaction rules rather than accommodating them. We then wonder why there is a disconnect. The assumption that autistic individuals' behaviors show diminished social desire or need, simply because they don't follow our social expectations, has negative effects on how they are treated. Rather than seeing such behaviors as reasons not to engage with others, we should see them as signals that we might need to step out of our own comfort zones. We might need to make ourselves vulnerable to others and learn from them. We need to stop expecting everyone to engage on terms that make us, not them, comfortable.

In general, people who are different from us make us uneasy. If we don't know people with a range of disabilities, disability will be unfamiliar to us. But then because of that unfamiliarity, we won't know how to engage people with disabilities. The cycle reinforces itself. The cultural pressure against those with disabilities is reinforced, even if we don't mean for it to be.

CHALLENGES IN THE CHURCH

Unfortunately, this cycle of uneasiness is often reinforced in the Church. In fact, one place that social exclusion is often the worst is church. People with disabilities are less likely to attend church regularly than are members of the nondisabled public. According to one survey, adults with disabilities in the US were almost 40% more likely never to attend a church, synagogue, or other place of worship. The more severe the disability, the less likely the person will be involved in a worshiping community. More than half of parents of children with disabilities report that their children have been excluded at church because of their disability. The odds of a child with autism never attending a religious service are double what they are for the general population. Disabilities that affect social interaction make people feel less welcome in places of worship than do physical disabilities, such as blindness or epilepsy, or chronic health concerns.

One reason for this is the Church's long history of ableism, some of which was discussed in chapter 2. Too often the Church's message regarding disability has been presented in ways that are overly simplistic, patronizing, or offensive to people with disabilities. As with mental illness, there is a strong stigma involved when the disability (or mental illness) is seen as related to a lack of faith or caused by sin.

I recently heard a sermon that criticized the ways that disability is often denigrated in church. However, during that sermon, the pastor still used "lame" as a term of derision to describe someone who dresses in socially disapproved ways. When he said this, there were three people in the congregation in wheelchairs, at least two using walkers, and one who has trouble walking because he lost a leg in war. Churches often don't know how to talk about disability, in part because it sits in tension with a God who, sometimes, heals.

Liz Bloomer works with people with disabilities, is the mother of a child with disabilities, and has struggled herself with disabling depression. She writes, "I consider church to be the one place where everyone should be welcome and I believe that fellowship, care and support is fundamental to church life." But it is often not like that.

CONCLUSION

The past three chapters have outlined the breadth of challenges that people with disabilities face. Some challenges are legal and political. Some are personal. And some are part of general social patterns. It is not always easy to read about these challenges, nor is it easy to live with them every day. But recognizing the challenges can equip us to do something about them.

So in the final chapter, I turn toward positive suggestions for making the various communities we are a part of more inclusive. And while much of this book has been aimed at anyone willing to think about such things, parts of the last chapter are specifically for those who are Christians. There I want to think about how Christians, both inside their churches and outside them, can make their communities more inclusive.

Moving Forward

6

We have come to the last chapter of this book. I hope you have learned something about disabilities and their impact on the lives of the people who have them. I have tried not to overload you with statistics. Percentages and demographic data don't make for the most gripping of reads. But the data is important, in part because many of us have wrong ideas about disabilities. And having the wrong ideas impacts our ability to improve things as we go forward.

Think about this misunderstanding. Only 17% of people with disabilities are born with them; the other 83% acquire them. Over 90% of people with disabilities are adults. However, when we think of disability, we often think of children. In my experience, most churches that have a disability ministry think of it primarily as oriented toward children with disabilities. Adults with disabilities, as mentioned earlier, often feel left out.

Or if we don't think of children, we think of people who use wheelchairs or other mobility aids. But only 7% of the disabled population in the US has a mobility impairment that requires the use of a wheelchair, walker, or cane. In contrast, over 70% of people who have a disability have an invisible disability—a disability that we wouldn't notice just by looking at them, such as attention-deficit/hyperactivity disorder (ADHD) or disabling depression.

We often think people with disabilities—since some of them are dependent in ways that we aren't—don't have much to teach us. We see people with disabilities as objects of care. Or worse, we see them as burdens rather than as our equals.

I have tried to show how we need to rethink much of what our culture believes about disability. Instead of making the person the problem, we need to identify the barriers that exclude and harm them. We need to make our communities more than just accessible for people with disabilities. We need to make them truly hospitable. We need to stop thinking of people with disabilities as "them," as "other." We need to think of them primarily as human. As part of "us."

THE HUMAN EXPERIENCE OF DISABILITY

As a culture, we need to accept disabilities as part of the human experience rather than stigmatizing those who have them. We affirm our collective humanity when we realize that we are all dependent. We need to stop fearing dependence. Those of us who don't have a disability have far more in common with those who do than we would like to admit. This isn't to say that "we are all disabled," as I have heard a few people say. That diminishes the very real difficulties faced by people with disabilities and demeans the ways that they have been, and are still, mistreated.

Those of us who lack disabilities often think that inclusion is something we do for those who have disabilities. It is an act of service, an act of charity. But notice that the attitude expressed in these thoughts is exclusionary. When inclusion happens—when we find a way to truly include everyone in our communities, regardless of their disabilities—we see all of us as involved in a joint project. When we do this, we will see that the entire community benefits from inclusion, not just those with disabilities. We have an obligation to work toward inclusion. But in doing so, we will make our communities better for everyone, including ourselves.

People with disabilities, especially if they are pressing for justice, may seem to be frustrated. That is because they often are. But frustration isn't a sin, and it isn't always bad. Much of that frustration is the product of decades, if not centuries, of exclusion. As we have seen, that exclusion isn't just a relic of the past. The effects of daily exclusion can be cumulative. Daily frustrations build up. You may not think it is a big deal to park in an accessible parking space "just for a few minutes." You may not think it is a big deal when your business doesn't have a van accessible parking space with the required 96-inch access aisle for wheelchair accessible vans. But if you have to deal with a lack of appropriate parking each time you go out, the frustration mounts. You may not think it is a big deal that insurance covers fifty-two weeks of medication per year but only thirty weeks of therapy. However, if you or a loved one needs that therapy just as much as others need the covered medication, you are likely to be frustrated by a system that seems rigged against disability.

Or consider the dearth of people with disabilities on television or in the movies. When they are present, they are too often portrayed by actors without disabilities. This is referred to as "cripping up" and reduces the number of roles for people with disabilities. As we saw in the previous chapter, people with disabilities are already underemployed. Furthermore, the ways that disability is often portrayed are problematic. Cultural perceptions of the badness of disability permeate much of our media. Popular movies such as *Million Dollar Baby* and *Me Before You* suggest that it is better to die than to live with a disability. Dory, from Disney's *Finding Nemo* and *Finding Dory*, is portrayed as a laughingstock or the object of pity because of her disability. Representation matters.

Disability is part of many people's lives. It is part of their identity, as I am sure it is for some of you reading this book. Disability isn't something to be ashamed of or to hide. Disability doesn't mean people need to be pitied. It is not better to be dead than disabled. Our discomfort is rooted in a negative reaction to disability. We shouldn't expect people to hide their experiences for our comfort. In fact, for our own well-being, we need to be made to confront our discomfort. But we also shouldn't reduce others' identities to just their disability. All of us are more than just one part of our identities.

Disability can shape the self-understanding of an entire family. Our daughters have been shaped by their experiences with their older brother. They see disability as a normal part of life. They talk about people having autism and using wheelchairs in heaven. But they are also more perceptive of the ways that other people can exclude individuals with disabilities than are many adults.

But family experiences aren't always positive. Many parents of children with disabilities talk about their struggles. And while those struggles should be acknowledged, care needs to be taken. One reason is that all parents struggle at times. There is a way of telling the stories that further marginalizes the children those stories are about. Well-meaning parents can do things that harm their children. They have. Many of their narratives suggest that disability is negative in a way that people with those disabilities deny. (Here I am thinking especially, though not only, of children with autism.) And those stories are told by parents. There is a long history of people with disabilities not being able to tell their own stories. These are reasons why, as indicated in the first chapter, I have tried to be very careful in presenting our own family story. I hope and pray that I have struck the right balance.

THINGS ARE COMPLICATED

In talking about our own family experience, I have had to oversimplify much of what we have been through. In fact, just about every discussion in this book is oversimplified. The issues are more complex than I have had time to discuss. There isn't a single experience of what it means to have a disability. Even different people with the same disability can have very different experiences. We need to engage with people with disabilities at all stages of our thinking about disability. We need to understand the breadth of their experiences. But that requires listening. And we can't listen to those we are not engaged with. We can't listen to those who aren't part of our lives.

I think that even the question of what counts as a disability is a more complicated question than we often think. The exact lines of disability are blurry, and making generalizations about disability as a whole is difficult. There is also great variation within the category of disability. Trying to address one kind of disability without acknowledging this diversity can cause us to exclude other kinds of disabilities by our very attempt to be inclusive. As I have said before, good intentions are important. But they aren't enough. As with dealing with the history of sexism, racism, and colonialism in the US and in the Church, addressing the harms, both past and present, related to disability will take time. It will require a radical and deliberate reorientation of our communities. It will require repentance and confession. I think most people don't try to exclude individuals with disabilities. They often just don't think about disability. Or if they do, they don't know how to begin addressing the interpersonal, structural, and political challenges. They might try, but they are afraid of getting it wrong. When they get it wrong, they are reluctant to try again. But we have to be willing to keep doing the work needed to transform our communities.

The patterns of exclusion I have discussed in the previous chapters suggest an additional injustice. The work of addressing the injustices our society imposes on those with disabilities is disproportionately borne by those who suffer those injustices. The disability rights movement was led primarily by those who had disabilities. Parents of students with disabilities have to be the primary advocates to get schools to follow the law. Families with members who have disabilities are often the ones who work to make their churches more inclusive.

Yet we can't simply outsource the work to those who have disabilities and their families. People with disabilities need to be present. They need to be welcome. They need to be valued. They need to be listened to. They need to be given the opportunity to lead. But then the rest of us need to come alongside them to do the work that is needed to transform our communities. Rather than being strangers we at best tolerate, individuals with disabilities should be people whose lives we are deeply and richly invested in. As Jean Vanier writes, "each of us needs to belong, not just to one person but to a family, friends, a group, and a culture."

A SPECIFIC CHALLENGE FOR THE CHURCH

I think all of us can benefit from these discussions. And while I don't want to limit the remaining few pages to those readers who are Christian, I think Christians have additional reasons to care about working toward inclusion. We, specifically, need to do better. We are called to be salt and light. And we have failed in this task.

The Church's focus shouldn't be just on cures or prayers for healing. Our focus shouldn't even be just on ministering *to* those with disabilities. It should be on ministering *with* those with disabilities. As my friend and disability advocate Barbara Newman says, "prepositions matter." Our focus should be on loving all those we encounter and on enabling others to love and be loved. We need to fold all of God's people into a community where they are valued and can be of value to others.

Part of being valued is being allowed the opportunity for leadership. Even in churches where individuals with disabilities are welcome, they are often excluded from positions of leadership or ministry. Here again I am reminded of the disability rights slogan "nothing about us without us." We need to take steps to correct this exclusion. God's work is done by those with disabilities.

The Church ought to be a beacon of inclusion. It ought to be a place where we can come together as a whole body, united in spirit and love for the good of all. It is together, collectively, that we are made holy. It is together that we are conformed into the image of Christ. And this is something that all of us—indeed, all of creation—contributes to.

Unfortunately, the Church often isn't the source of the Good News that it claims to proclaim. As theologian John Hull writes, "churches have become reflections of the world of capitalist economies." They all too often reflect the same structural patterns of exclusion that we see in the larger culture. The Church, like the larger culture, often focuses less on inclusion than it does on the pragmatics involved in adding new programs. The Church, like the larger culture, often can't find the financial resources for inclusion (when it can find the resources for all sorts of other programming). The Church, like the larger culture, is often unwilling to take the time to slow down the pace of life in the way needed to include many who have disabilities that demand extra time. The Church, like the larger culture, doesn't seek out the voices of individuals with disabilities to do things *with* them; it would often rather do things *for* individuals with disabilities—even though those efforts are often misguided precisely because they lack the voices of those excluded. Although the Church recognizes in its theology that we are dependent on one another and on God, too often it acts as if dependency is a problem to be solved rather than an inherent human trait to be affirmed and even celebrated.

Even in the Church, we often think of people as commodities to be traded, with one person's interests needing to be weighed against another's. Decisions come down to balancing special interests against special interests. With such a mind-set, it is almost impossible for vulnerable people not to be marginalized. (And remember, we are all vulnerable.) What is left out is an overarching commitment to the *common* good.

We are often uncomfortable with people criticizing the Church. Calling out that our churches are often just as exclusionary as the wider culture is the voice crying in the wilderness, a voice that is not appreciated. If the Church responds with the call to "play nice" or "just be patient," that voice crying out for justice is further marginalized. As with minority voices calling out for racial justice, when persons with disabilities call out to be recognized in their full humanity, the Church needs to listen.

Christians should default to listening to the oppressed. We should make sure our priorities reflect the kingdom initiated by our Christ. We should embrace the very dependency that we too often run from. We need to work to realize a new vision of community, one grounded in the vision of the kingdom of God. To quote theologian Amos Yong, we need to work toward community in which "people with disabilities are . . . accepted, included, and valued members of the human family regardless of how they measure up to our economic, social, and political conventions."

Remember, more than 20% of the general population has a disability. You may be among them. But if you are not, and if you don't have friends or family members with disabilities, you may be doing something to exclude them from your life. Even if you don't mean to. So go find them. Befriend them. Listen to them and learn from them. Draw close to them. Sit with them. Walk the slow walk with them. Invest in their lives and let them invest in yours. Support their ordination. Build the kingdom with them. For when we do this, we all benefit.

Notes

Series Editor's Foreword

9 **Midway along the journey of our life:** the opening verse of Dante Alighieri, *The Inferno*, trans. Mark Musa (Bloomington: Indiana University Press, 1995), 19.

10 **"We are always on the road":** from Calvin's thirty-fourth sermon on Deuteronomy (5:12–14), preached on June 20, 1555 (*Ioannis Calvini Opera quae supersunt Omnia*, ed. Johann-Wilhelm Baum et al. [Brunsvigae: C. A. Schwetschke et Filium, 1883], 26.291), as quoted in Herman Selderhuis, *John Calvin: A Pilgrim's Life* (Downers Grove, IL: InterVarsity, 2009), 34.

10 **"a gift of divine kindness":** from the last chapter of John Calvin, *Institutes of the Christian Religion, 1541 French Edition*, trans. Elsie Anne McKee (Grand Rapids: Eerdmans, 2009), 704. Titled "Of the Christian Life," the entire chapter is a guide to wise and faithful living in this world.

Chapter 1

20 **When Jameson was five years old:** my interview for *This Little Miss Miggy Stayed Home* can be found at http://www.this littlemiggy.com/2012/11/special-needs-spotlight-jameson.html.

27 **"The popular image of autism":** Kerry Magro, foreword to *I Am Strong: The Life and Journey of an Autistic Pastor*, by Lamar Hardwick (Little Elm, TX: eLectio Publishing, 2018), v.

29 **In his book *I Am Strong*:** the first quotation comes page 5, the second from page 2.

Chapter 2

34 **"Understanding dementia is a bit like":** John Swinton, *Dementia: Living in the Memories of God* (Grand Rapids: Eerdmans, 2012), 27.

35 **"We need honesty to meet":** Matthew C. Halteman, *Compassionate Eating as Care of Creation*, http://www.humanesociety. org/assets/pdfs/faith/compassionate_eating_halteman_book. pdf, 3.

37 **But other parts of the New Testament:** a discussion of how the New Testament often reinforces the belief that disability must be cured can be found in Amos Yong, *Theology and Down Syndrome: Reimagining Disability in Late Modernity* (Waco: Baylor University Press, 2007), chapter 2.

37 **Many Christians in the medieval period:** a discussion of the theory of maternal imagination can be found in Julia Epstein, "The Pregnant Imagination, Fetal Rights, and Women's Bodies: A Historical Inquiry," *Yale Journal of Law & the Humanities* 7, no. 1 (1995): 139–62.

38 **As Rebecca Chopp writes:** Rebecca S. Chopp, foreword to *The Disabled God: Toward a Liberatory Theology of Disability*, by Nancy L. Eiesland (Nashville: Abingdon Press, 1994), 11.

38 **Martin Luther, for example, referred to children with intellectual disabilities:** cited in Ronald J. Berger, *Introducing Disability Studies* (Boulder, CO: Lynne Rienner Publishers, 2013), 54.

38 **Leo X, who was pope:** the story about Pope Leo is from R. C. Scheerenberger, *A History of Mental Retardation* (Baltimore: Brookes Publishing, 1983), 33f.

40 **The first code of laws:** *The Body of Liberties* and special education in the early history of the United States are discussed in Scheerenberger, *A History of Mental Retardation*, 92 and 166.

40 **In 1866, Edouard Seguin:** Edouard Seguin is discussed in James W. Trent Jr., *Inventing the Feeble Mind: A History of Mental Retardation in the United States* (Berkeley: University of California Press, 1994).

40 **However, for much of its history:** an extended discussion of the role of disability in US history, from which much of the information in this chapter is taken, can be found in Kim E. Nielsen, *A Disability History of the United States* (Boston: Beacon Press, 2013).

41 **In the early twentieth century:** the quotation is from 1917 instructions to immigration officials, which are discussed in Nielsen, *A Disability History of the United States*, 103.

41 **Economies of scale and concerns:** the phrase "ease of resident management" is from Scheerenberger, *A History of Mental Retardation*, 193.

42 **As one state-level administrator noted:** Scheerenberger, *A History of Mental Retardation*, 252.

42 **In 1966, Barton Blatt and Fred Kaplan:** The essay is available in book form in Barton Blatt and Fred Kaplan, *Christmas in Purgatory: A Photographic Essay on Mental Retardation* (Syracuse, NY: Human Policy Press, 1974).

42 **In 1972, investigative journalist Geraldo Rivera:** Geraldo Rivera's *Willowbrook: The Last Great Disgrace* was released by WABC-TV Channel 7 in 1972.

43 **Supreme Court Justice Oliver Wendell Holmes Jr.:** the *Buck v. Bell* case, and the subsequent history of forced sterilizations of individuals with disabilities, can be found in Paul A. Lombardo, *Three Generations, No Imbeciles: Eugenics, the Supreme Court, and Buck v. Bell* (Baltimore: Johns Hopkins University Press, 2008).

43 **For instance, Samuel Cartwright:** the quotation is from Samuel Cartwright's 1848 "The Diseased and Physical Peculiarities of the Negro Race," which is discussed in Nielsen, *A Disability History of the United States*, 57.

44 **The term *mongoloid*:** a discussion of the racist origins of the term "mongoloid" as a reference to Down syndrome can be found in Yong, *Theology and Down Syndrome*, 49.

44 **In the 1980s, the American Lutheran Church:** the American Lutheran Church's use of disability to exclude from ordination is discussed in Eiesland, *The Disabled God*, chapters 4 and 6.

Chapter 3

49 **Section 504 of the Rehabilitation Act in 1973:** this can be found at https://www.dol.gov/oasam/regs/statutes/sec504.htm.

49 **the Americans with Disabilities Act (ADA) in 1990:** this can be found at https://www.ada.gov/ada_intro.htm.

49 **the Individuals with Disabilities Education Act (IDEA) in 1990:** this can be found at https://sites.ed.gov/idea/.

49 **Vic Finkelstein, himself disabled by a spinal cord injury:** Finkelstein's story "To Deny or Not to Deny Disability" can be found at https://www.independentliving.org/docs1/finkel-stein.html.

55 **In 1981, Evan J. Kemp Jr. wrote an op-ed:** Kemp's op-ed, titled "Aiding the Disabled: No Pity, Please," can be found at https://www.nytimes.com/1981/09/03/opinion/aiding-the-disabled-no-pity-please.html.

Chapter 4

64 **In the *Washington Post*, Lennard Davis and David Perry:** Davis and Perry's piece, "Protecting the Rights of People with Disabilities Is Not Optional," can be found at https://www.washingtonpost.com/opinions/protecting-the-rights-of-people-with-disabilities-is-not-optional/2017/09/26/.

66 **At the 2009 Special Olympics World Winter Games:** information about the "Spread the Word to End the Word" campaign can be found at https://www.r-word.org/.

69 **As theologian John Swinton says:** Swinton, *Dementia*, 135.

73 **Theologian John Swinton uses the phrase:** Swinton, *Dementia*, 84.

Chapter 5

80 **The 2016 Disability Statistics Annual Report**: Lewis Kraus, *2016 Disability Statistics Annual Report* (Durham, NH: University of New Hampshire, 2017). The report may be accessed at https://disabilitycompendium.org/annualreport.

80 **Companies such as Goodwill:** a discussion of Goodwill and minimum wage for workers with disabilities can be found at https://www.forbes.com/sites/susanadams/2013/07/30/does -goodwill-industries-exploit-disabled-workers/#54d3c2 036a56 and https://www.motherjones.com/politics/2017/08 /many-people-with-disabilities-are-being-paid-way-below -the-minimum-wage-and-its-perfectly-legal/.

81 **According to the Census Bureau**: data on citizens with disabilities may be accessed at https://www.census.gov/topics/health /disability.html.

81 **This illustrates *intersectionality:*** Kimberlé Crenshaw's use of the term intersectionality is discussed at https://www .newstatesman.com/lifestyle/2014/04/kimberl-crenshaw -intersectionality-i-wanted-come-everyday-metaphor -anyone-could.

82 **Awareness of these issues:** the website for Sevy's paintings can be found at https://www.sevymarieart.com/.

85 **According to the British National Health Service:** data may be found at https://obgyn.onlinelibrary.wiley.com/doi/ pdf/10.1111/j.1471-0528.1995.tb11315.x

85 **However, abortion rates:** the increase in abortion rates since the passage of the ADA is discussed in Dov Fox and Christopher L. Griffin Jr., "Disability-Selective Abortion and the

Americans with Disabilities Act," available at https://core
.ac.uk/download/pdf/73972219.pdf.

85 **In 2015, college students studying nursing and other
    health professions:** the study can be found in Frida Simon-
    stein and Michal Mashiach-Eizenberg, "Attitudes Toward
    Autism Spectrum Disorders Among Students of Allied
    Health Profession," *Journal of Genetic Counseling* 35 (2016):
    1276–85.

89 **"The shared pain and the place":** Jean Vanier and John
    Swinton, *Mental Health: The Inclusive Church Resource* (Lon-
    don: Darton, Longman and Todd, 2014), 58.

89 **In his book *The Enabled Life:*** Roy McCloughry, *The Enabled
    Life: Christianity in a Disabling World* (London: SPCK Pub-
    lishing, 2013), 1.

93 **She writes, "I consider church to be":** Vanier and Swinton,
    Mental Health, 31.

Chapter 6

103 **As Jean Vanier writes:** Jean Vanier, *Becoming Human* (Mah-
    wah, NY: Paulist Press, 1998), 33.

104 **As my friend and disability advocate Barbara Newman
    says:** Newman's statement that "prepositions matter" can be
    found in the video "Disability in Heaven," available at https://
    www.youtube.com/watch?v=eIE1kYqfKhE.

105 **As theologian John Hull writes:** John Hull, *Disability: The
    Inclusive Church Resource* (London: Darton, Longman and
    Todd, 2014), 94.

106 **To quote theologian Amos Yong:** Yong, *Theology and Down
    Syndrome*, 182.

For Further Reading

I recommend the following books, which nicely complement the topics and issues covered in each chapter.

Chapter 1

Shakespeare, Tom. *Disability: The Basics*. New York: Routledge, 2017.

Yancey, Hilary. *Forgiving God: A Story of Faith*. New York: Faith-Words, 2018.

Chapter 2

Brock, Brian, and John Swinton, eds. *Disability in the Christian Tradition: A Reader*. Grand Rapids, MI: Eerdmans, 2012.

Nielsen, Kim E. *A Disability History of the United States*. Boston: Beacon Press, 2013.

Chapter 3

Davis, Lennard J. *Enabling Acts: The Hidden Story of How the Americans with Disabilities Act Gave the Largest US Minority Its Rights*. Boston: Beacon Press, 2015.

Shapiro, Joseph P. *No Pity: People with Disabilities Forging a New Civil Rights Movement*. New York: Three Rivers Press, 1993.

Chapter 4

Kim, Cynthia. *Nerdy, Shy, and Socially Inappropriate: A User Guide to an Asperger Life*. London: Jessica Kingsley Publishers, 2015.

Wilder, Courtney. *Disability, Faith, and the Church: Inclusion and Accommodation in Contemporary Congregations*. Santa Barbara, CA: Praeger, 2016.

Chapter 5

Bascom, Julia. *Loud Hands: Autistic People, Speaking*. Washington, DC: The Autistic Press, 2012.

Brown, Lydia X. Z., E. Ashkenazy, and Morénike Giwa Onaiwu, eds. *All the Weight of Our Dreams: On Living Racialized Autism*. Lincoln, NE: DragonBee Press, 2017.

Chapter 6

Carter, Erik W. *Including People with Disabilities in Faith Communities: A Guide for Service Providers, Families, and Congregations*. Baltimore, MD: Paul H. Brookes Publishing, 2007.

Hull, John. *Disability: The Inclusive Church Resource*. London: Darton, Longman and Todd, 2014.

Newman, Barbara J. *Accessible Gospel, Inclusive Worship*. Wyoming, MI: CLC Network, 2015.